Print Writing

Practice Book

Flash Kids

A Division of Barnes & Noble Publishing

Harcourt Family Learning™

© 2004 by Flsh Kids
Adapted from *Write-On, Wipe-Off Handwriting: Manuscript* by M.C. Hall
© 2001 by Harcourt Achieve Inc.
Licensed under special arrangement with Harcourt Achieve Inc.

ISBN: 978-1-4114-0087-0

Please submit all inquiries to FlashKids@bn.com

Printed and bound in China

Flash Kids
A Division of Barnes & Noble
122 Fifth Avenue
New York, NY 10011

Dear Parent,

Even in the age of computers, good handwriting is a must! This book provides an easy and enjoyable way for your child to learn to write manuscript letters and numbers. More than 100 practice pages provide ample opportunity for your child to master the manuscript alphabet and begin writing words and sentences. The fun animal facts and vivid illustrations throughout the book will hold your child's interest as he or she develops these new skills.

Each letter of the alphabet is presented on four pages. Your child will learn how to form each letter, and then practice the letter several times before moving on to words and simple sentences.

To help your child get the most from this book, follow these simple teaching tips:

- Before your child begins a new letter, demonstrate how to write it on a large piece of paper. Show your child how to make each stroke.

- Have your child trace the letter in the air with his or her index finger.

- Remind your child to use the directional arrows as cues for where to begin each part of the letter.

- Remember that practice makes perfect. Encourage your child to write each letter until he or she feels comfortable.

For added value, the pictures and facts in this book can be used to extend your child's learning. Consider some of these activities:

- Use this book's alphabetical format to reinforce letter sequencing. Ask your child to find specific letter pages.

- Use the animal names to help teach and practice letter sounds. Discuss the initial sound of each animal's name. Ask your child to think of other words that begin with the same sound.

- Read the fun fact about each animal. Consult nonfiction books or the Internet to find out more about the creatures shown on these pages.

A a

A A A A A A A

a a a a a a

A A A A A A A A A A A

a a a a a a a a a a a a a

Ant Ant Ant Ant Ant

Ant Ant Ant Ant Ant

ant ant ant ant

ant ant ant ant

ant ant ant ant

FUN FACT

An ant can carry something bigger than its body!

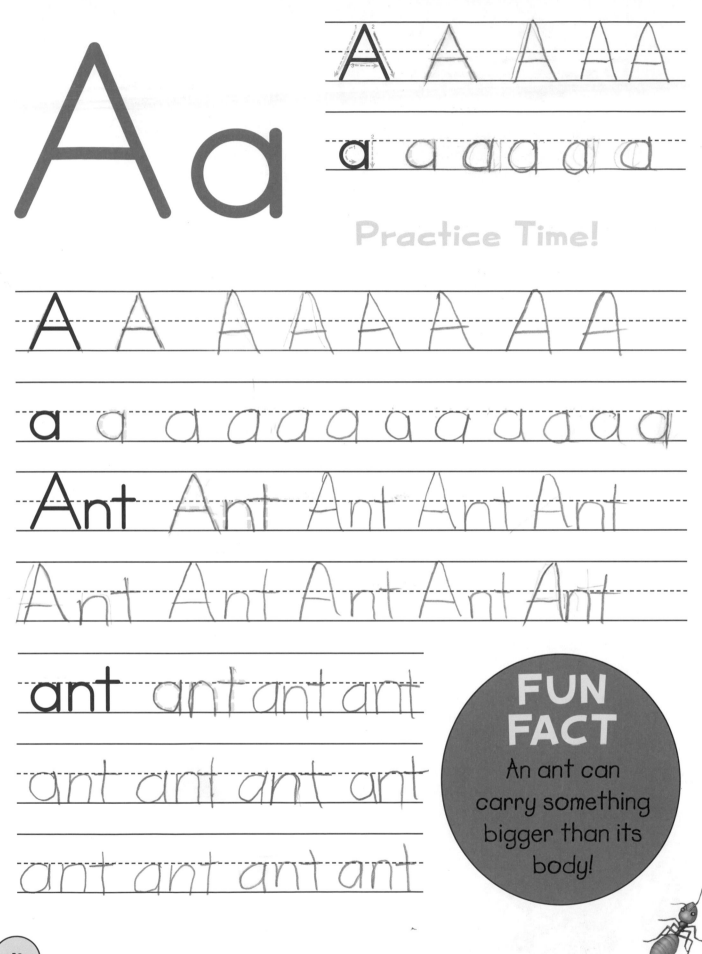

4

Ants eat leaves.

Ants eat leaves.

Ants eat leaves.

Ants eat leaves.

Ants are small.

Ants are small.

A a

A A A A A A A

a a a a a a a

A a A a A a A a A a A

April April April April

April April April April

animal animal animal

animal

at

Now write your own words.

B b

B B

b b

B B

b b

Bear Bear

bear bear

FUN FACT

Baby bears are born in the winter.

8

Bear cubs play.

Bear cubs sleep.

Bb

B B

b b

B b

Brian

ball

bug

Now write your own words.

C c

C C C C

C C

c c

Cat Cat

cat cat

FUN FACT

Cats can see
in the dark.

Cats chase mice.

Cats are cute.

C c

C C C C

c c c

C c

Canada

child

car

Now write your own words.

D d

D

d

Duck

duck

FUN FACT

Ducks have webbed feet.

16

Ducks can swim.

Ducks like water.

D d

D D

d d

Dd

Daddy

day

dog

Now write your own words.

E e

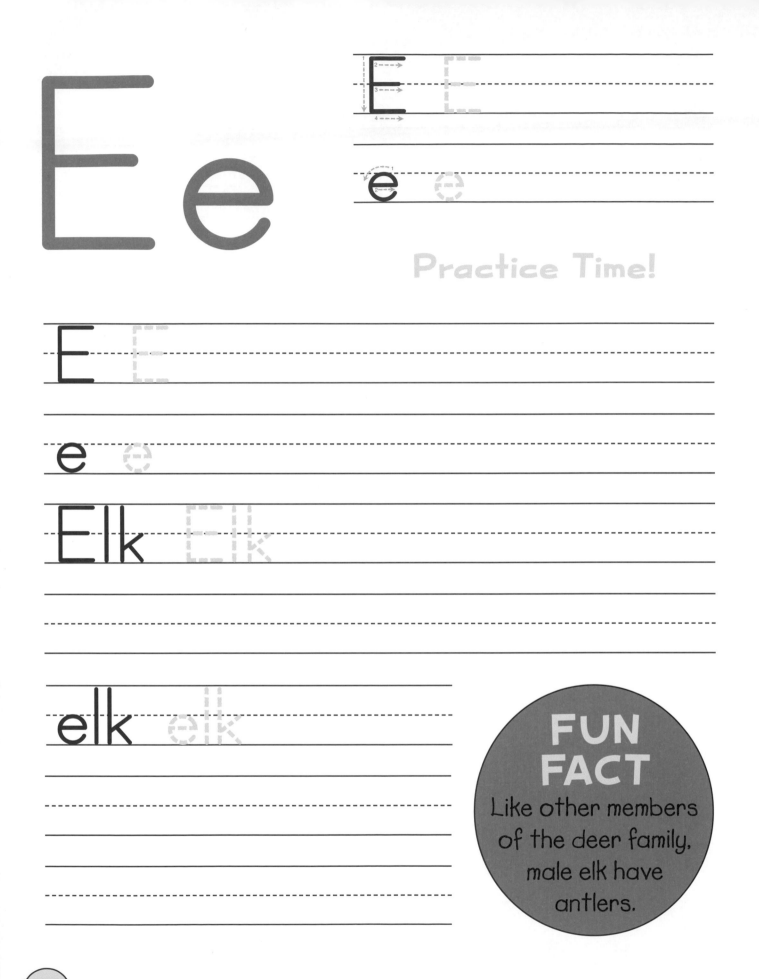

E E

e e

E E

e e

Elk Elk

elk elk

FUN FACT
Like other members of the deer family, male elk have antlers.

Elk eat leaves.

Elk are like deer.

E e

E E E

e e

E e

Earth

elephant

eel

Now write your own words.

F f

Practice Time!

F

f

Fox

fox

FUN FACT

The fox is a member of the dog family.

24

Foxes are fast.

Foxes are furry.

F f

F F

f f

F f

Friday

fifty

face

Now write your own words.

G g

G G

g g

G G

g g

Goat Goat

goat goat

FUN FACT

Goats can climb on rocks.

28

Goats eat grass.

Goats can be gray.

Gg

G G G

g g g

G g

Grandmother

going

girl

Now write your own words.

H h

H H H

h h h

Horse Horse

horse horse

FUN FACT

Horses are very smart animals.

Horses like hay.

Horses have hooves.

H h

H H

h h

H h

Hannah

heart

half

Now write your own words.

I i

I I

i i

Iguana Iguana

iguana iguana

FUN FACT

Many iguanas have spikes down their backs.

Iguanas are lizards.

Iguanas eat insects.

I i

I I

i i

I i

Iris

inside

it

Now write your own words.

J j

J

j

Jaguar

jaguar

FUN FACT

The jaguar's long whiskers help it to move in the dark.

Jaguars can jump.

Jaguars live in jungles.

J j

J   J   J

j   j   j

J j

June

juice

jar

Now write your own words.

K k

K

k

Koala

koala

FUN FACT

Koalas carry their babies on their backs.

44

Koalas like leaves.

Koalas climb quickly.

K k

K K

k k

K k

Kenya

kind

kid

Now write your own words.

L l

L

l

Lion Lion

lion lion

FUN FACT

A lion family is called a pride.

48

Lions like sunlight.

Lion cubs play.

L l

L L

I l

L l

Lily

large

lovely

Now write your own words.

M m

M M M

m m

Practice Time!

M M

m m

Manatee Manatee

manatee

manatee

FUN FACT

The manatee is also called a "sea cow."

52

Manatees are gray.

Manatees have fins.

M m

M M

m m

M m

Monday

mailman

mat

Now write your own words.

N n

N

n

Newt

newt

FUN FACT

A newt spends most of its time in the water.

Newts can swim.

Newts have long tails.

N n

N N N

n n

N n

November

nineteen

nice

Now write your own words.

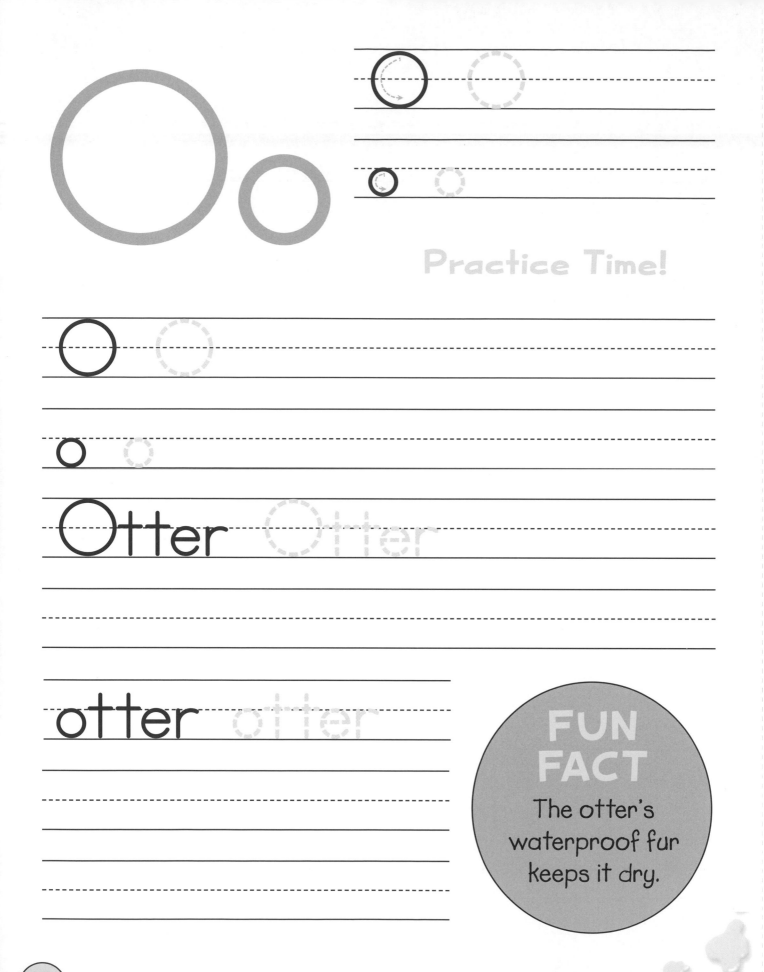

Practice Time!

Otter   Otter

otter   otter

FUN FACT

The otter's waterproof fur keeps it dry.

60

Otters love water.

Otters eat frogs.

O o

October

octopus

onto

Now write your own words.

P p

P

P

p

Pig

pig

FUN FACT

Baby pigs are called piglets.

64

Pigs live in pens.

Pigs play in mud.

P p

P   P   P

p   p   p

P p

Pluto

people

pal

Now write your own words.

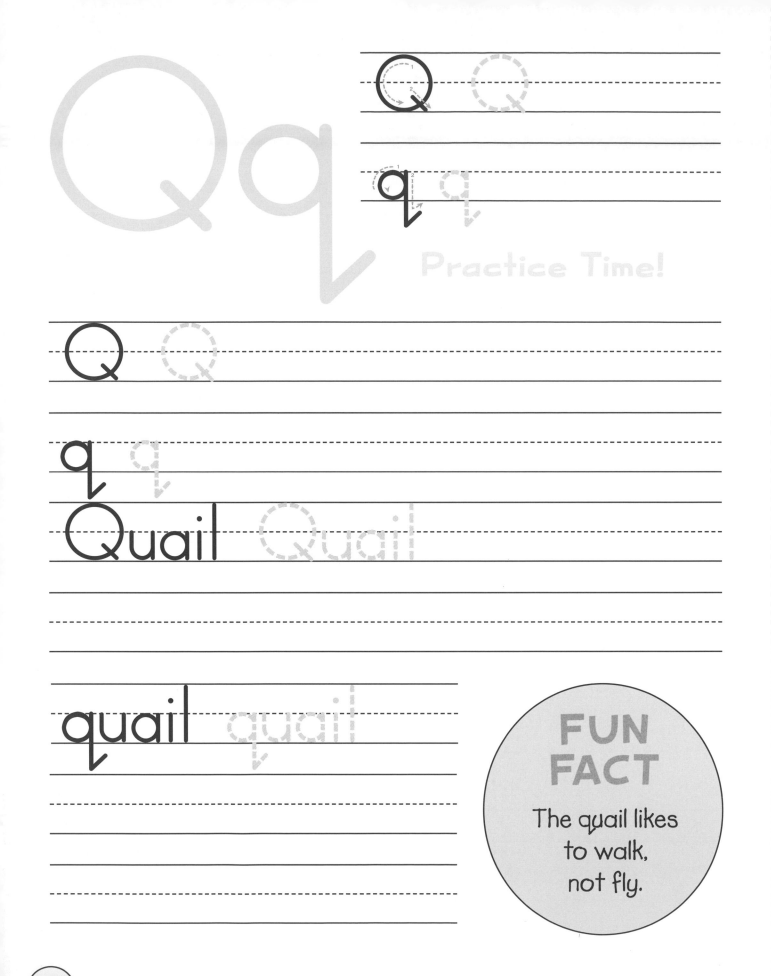

Q q

Practice Time!

Q Q

q q

Quail Quail

quail quail

FUN FACT

The quail likes to walk, not fly.

Quail are quiet.

Quail do not quack.

Q q

Q Q

q q

Q q

Queen

quiet

quarter

R r

R R

r r

R R

r r

Rabbit Rabbit

rabbit rabbit

FUN FACT

Rabbits have big back feet.

Rabbits can run.

Rabbits eat radishes.

R r

R R

r r

R r

Robert

reindeer

river

Now write your own words.

S s

S s

S S

s s

Seal Seal

seal seal

FUN FACT

Baby seals are called pups.

Seals can swim.

Seals eat small fish.

S s

S S

s s

S s

Saturday

sister

socks

Now write your own words.

T t

Practice Time!

T T

t t

Tiger Tiger

tiger tiger

FUN FACT

A tiger's stripes help it hide!

80

Tigers have tails.

Tigers hunt at night.

T t

T T

t t

T t

Tuesday

tight

twenty

Now write your own words.

U u

Practice Time!

Umbrella Bird

umbrella bird

FUN FACT

The umbrella bird lives in the rain forest.

84

Umbrella birds fly.

Umbrella birds sing.

U u

U   u

u   u

U u

Uncle

under

usual

Now write your own words.

V v

V V

v v

Vole Vole

vole vole

FUN FACT

Voles live underground.

88

Voles are very little.

Voles have fur.

V v

V V

v v

V v

Venus

velvet

vest

Now write your own words.

Ww

W

w

Warthog

warthog

FUN FACT

The warthog lives on the grassy plains of Africa.

92

Warthogs are wild.

Warthogs have tusks.

Ww

W w

W w

Wednesday

window

was

Now write your own words.

X x

X X

x x

X-ray Fish X-ray Fish

x-ray fish

x-ray fish

FUN FACT

It looks like you can see inside an X-ray fish.

96

X-ray fish are small.

X-ray fish have fins.

X x

X x

X x

X ray

xylophone

exit

Y y

Y y

Y

y

Yak

yak

FUN FACT

Yaks live in the mountains.

100

Yaks have fur.

Yaks are very shaggy.

Y y

Y Y

y y

Y y

Yolanda

young

yard

Now write your own words.

Z z

Practice Time!

Z Z

z z

Zebra Zebra

zebra zebra

FUN FACT

Every zebra looks different.

104

Zebras eat grass.

Zebras have stripes.

Zz

Z Z

z z

Z z

Zack

zipper

zero

Now write your own words.

1

2

3

4

5

Count the animals. Write the number.

six

ten

four

eight

seven

6 6

7 7

8 8

9 9

10 10

Count the animals. Write the number.

two

five

three

nine

one

Match each animal to its home.

bird

den

bee

house

bear

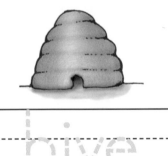

hive

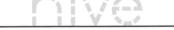

dog

nest

Match each animal to its baby.

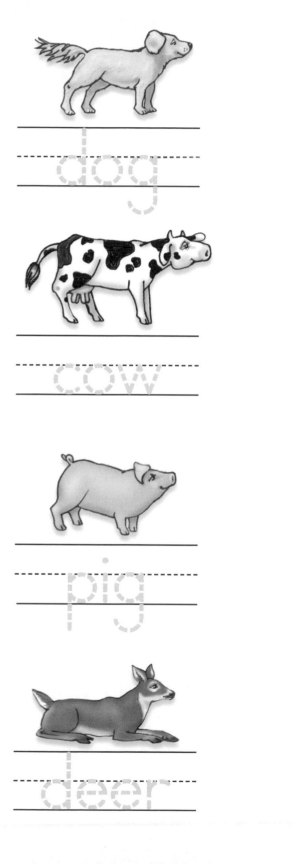

dog

pup

cow

piglet

pig

fawn

deer

calf

111

More Practice!

Aa   Bb

Cc   Dd   Ee   Ff

Gg   Hh   Ii   Jj

Kk   Ll   Mm   Nn

Oo   Pp   Qq   Rr

Ss   Tt   Uu   Vv

Ww   Xx   Yy   Zz